STUCK!

STUCK!

Break Out of Your Emotional Prison

and Get On With Your Life

BY JOHN VOLKMAR

© 2006 John Volkmar
All Rights Reserved.

No part of this publication may be reproduced, stored in a retrieval system, or transmitted, in any form or by any means, electronic, mechanical, photocopying, recording, or otherwise, without the written permission of the author.

First published by Dog Ear Publishing
4010 W. 86th Street, Ste H
Indianapolis, IN 46268
www.dogearpublishing.net

ISBN: 1-59858-235-6
Library of Congress Control Number: 2006936071

This book is printed on acid-free paper.

Printed in the United States of America

DEDICATION

To Buere, with love and gratitude

CONTENTS

About John Volkmar ix

Opening Thoughts xi

Chapter 1: How Did I Get Here? 1

Chapter 2: Letting Go 15

Chapter 3: Moving On 21

Chapter 4: The Probation Officer 29

Chapter 5: Love Thyself 37

Chapter 6: Who Needs Expectations? 47

Chapter 7: Meet Your Higher Self 53

Chapter 8: Putting It All Together 61

Chapter 9: Have Fun! 69

Chapter 10: A Review 73

Appendices: Creative Visualization 81

The Good and Bad Stress 87

ABOUT JOHN VOLKMAR

John Volkmar has been focused on a spiritual path since 1954, studying, experiencing and teaching the steps leading to spiritual fulfillment. Today, both as a teacher and student, he continues his search for universal truths while helping clients take responsibility for their lives and achieve an inner tranquility and high level of wellness.

His search has taken him to many parts of the world. He and his wife Joanne organized educational and development projects in North and West Africa, the Middle East and Asia. In West Africa, the Middle East and at the United Nations, he initiated and participated in peacemaking efforts between nations at war and between liberation groups and governments in power. He has written and published articles on these subjects, as well as coauthoring a challenging book called *The Middle East and a New Realism* with General Indar Rikhye, then Director of the International Peace Academy. He also wrote a book on peace options for the Middle East conflict for IDOC called *Geneva or Elsewhere*. He testified in the House of Representatives and the Senate in Washington, proposing steps toward peace on behalf of world Quakers.

His recent book, entitled *On Becoming Powerful*, is published in four languages and continues to sell in Europe, Latin America and the United States. The book is an easy-to-read and follow manual for achieving personal fulfillment, controlling stress and maintaining a state of high-level wellness.

The theme of John's life has been to guide individuals, communities and nations who feel powerless to develop their inherent strengths in order to improve their lives. In his work today as a holistic teacher and spiritual coach with individuals and groups, the emphasis is the same. When you take responsibility for yourself physically, mentally and spiritually, true wellness will be experienced. He teaches self-healing skills, how to avoid illness and recurrence of illness, life management skills, managing stress, techniques for building self-esteem, and how to use creative visualization to realize your goals in everyday life and in business.

In each of his video and audio CDs, you will have an opportunity to participate along with the other students in one of his life-changing workshops.

BREAK OUT

OF YOUR EMOTIONAL PRISON

and GET ON WITH YOUR LIFE

YOU'RE OFF ON A WONDERFUL JOURNEY!
OPENING THOUGHTS

A couple of years ago I offered a new workshop called JAIL-BREAK, with the subtitle of "It's easier to break out of jail than the prison of your own creation." It was not difficult to find twelve participants. The original plan was to have four two-hour sessions. However, as we progressed we discovered that we were overly optimistic and added two more sessions at the end. Part of the final session was taken up by participant critiques. We decided to meet together in three months and review our personal experiences during those months. Listing some of those critiques will be helpful to you, as this book follows the same program as the workshop.

"The processes and changes recommended by the course were sufficient to bring about positive change, however, some trial scenarios would have helped."

"I would have liked this workshop to go on longer."

"One of the [cell] bars I expressed was my detachment and aloofness. In the workshop I feel that I was able to engage and be a productive member of the group."

"I fully realize that what was started is a process that doesn't have a defined endpoint."

"It made great sense to me to identify a Probation Officer to meet with on a regular basis as I often start things and never finish them."

"Being challenged forced me to deal with issues that I have swept under the rug for years."

Let me add that in spite of the seriousness of our goals, we always found time for humor and laughter. I hope I can inject some in this book.

We met on a Sunday at the home of one of the participants. Before enjoying a delicious potluck lunch, we sat together and talked about the changes that we had gone through since the workshop. The consensus was that the workshop experience was positive. It seems that the participants had recognized positive changes in the quality of their lives. They felt better about themselves and felt more able to create a vision for a future direction. They urged me to write up the workshop in a manual so that more people could benefit from the process. So here goes.

During the years of growing up, we have many "unforgettable" and in some cases, forgettable experiences that are buried in our Long-Term Memory. There can also be heard messages that influence how we see ourselves. Parents may say, "You were an unexpected surprise, although we still love you as much as your sister." "You were a difficult birth. I guess you just didn't want to be born." "Your brother is smarter than you, but you will find your way." "In spite of your looks, someday you will find the ideal husband." Teachers sometimes say, "Too bad you are not as smart as your older sister." These messages continue throughout our growing-up years. (Let's hope that we are still growing up.)

Experiences, usually traumatic, involving losses or feelings of abandonment and betrayal, leave emotional scars that are in the (unconscious) Long-Term Memory. These influence how we react to events and challenges which we face in a normal day. Divorce, loss of grandparents and even a pet can have an influence. Pets give healing, unconditional love, which we almost never get from our parents or siblings. Many children turn to a pet for comfort after being punished or criticized.

As you begin working, more "forgotten" memorable events will surface. Other qualities that can play a role in blockage are perceptions, values, relationships and friends, and the home and work situation.

I assume that since you have read this far, you feel "stuck" and are ready to move. Here are some perceptions which you may relate to:

1. I am never lucky.
2. I just live day by day.
3. Most of my problems are rooted in my childhood.
4. I have low self-esteem.
5. I usually settle for less than the best.
6. I don't make any plans for the future.
7. I hate my job.
8. I have trouble accepting authority.
9. I don't experience any joy in my life.

10. I almost never finish anything I start.

11. I have trouble keeping my friends.

12. Some days, nothing is right.

Now remember some of the triumphs, successes of your life, some joyful moments. Remember times when you were a good friend to someone in need, when you achieved a goal that you set out for yourself or when a person congratulated you on a deed well done. All of these can support your self-esteem while you go through this process of liberation.

Several times in the book I will suggest the use of your journal, which is not a daily diary but a record of interesting memories and intuitive "ahaaas" that are bound to surface in your conscious mind during this exercise. In any exercise of introspection such as this one or even therapy, one spends a great part of the day remembering and searching the past. These flashes, which are often forgotten, are important to record in order that they can remain a part of this process.

Please buy a small spiral notebook or, if you want to get fancy, a nicely bound book of blank pages at a greeting card store. I specify small because it must be easy to carry around with you during the day.

While reading this brief introduction, many questions will come to mind. Be patient. As you proceed, the answers will appear. I have made an effort to make this manual easy to use, with exercises that are easy to follow. Doing these exercises is vital if you wish to have a successful experience and achieve your goals.

At the end of the book there are two sections: one to teach you the technique of Creative Visualization and the other makes suggestions on how to reduce stress in your life.

I'll meet you at Chapter One.

CHAPTER 1

HOW DID I GET HERE?

Welcome! Let's go to work.

What does your prison feel like? Do you feel hopeless? Defeated in advance? Are you undeserving of release, victimized and above all, tired? Maybe for months or even years you have wanted to feel free but never knew how to take the first step.

Count the cell bars and read the labels on them. Address one at a time.

At this point a "smart aleck" participant in the workshop raised his hand, saying "I'd get my girlfriend to send me a birthday cake with a hacksaw blade in it." Nobody laughed. As we proceeded with the workshop, his turned out to be one of the toughest cells to break out of. At some level he must have known of the rough road ahead.

CELL BARS NUMBER ONE AND TWO
Negative Personal Values and Perceptions

There is seldom a moment in your day when your personal values do not play a role in your actions, perceptions and responses to stimuli—probably less so during sleep. However, many of your dream themes involve protecting or asserting them.

I find that when I see a mother at the market stuff a doughnut into her whining child's mouth with no intention of paying for it, I am more concerned about the lesson she is teaching her child than her dishonesty. The child's learned perception is that it is okay to steal and eat food while shopping. This mother probably got her doughnut while shopping with her own mother. If in the past I found myself in the checkout line with her, I would remind her of the doughnut. Now I stay quiet, realizing that she is probably in a maximum-security prison cell.

Another perception or cell bar is that without a formal college education one can "never amount to anything." Many individuals, both men and women, who have propelled civilization forward by their "crazy" ideas, were considered crazy in the sense that they did not meet the approval of the scientific and academic communities. Even today, an unconventional cancer treatment is condemned by the medical establishment in spite of the fact that it has a substantial record of success. Many of these innovators were artists, political activists, tycoons, doctors and writers. One fine example of a crazy man was Leonardo de Vinci whose visions included helicopters, a robot and gear-driven machines. A collection of his inventions fills a museum in the town of Vinci in Italy. Dr. Salk, with medical training, was able to make a quantum leap by creating an infantile paralysis vaccine that saved millions of lives. One of the giant tycoons of the nineteenth century never went beyond the eighth grade in school. The message here is that perceptions can keep us from achieving our life purpose, and that the security a formal education offers by supporting our work with data or precedent may turn out to be a block to creative expression.

Another perception is that you do not take risks or a leap without knowing where you are going to land. This fear keeps you locked up and unable to "take a leap of faith." Often you find yourself looking over the edge of a cliff and seeing nothing below—no safe landing pad—so you back off. You do this several times before you realize that in order to move forward in your life you must jump. You jump and the landing is soft and you discover a whole new energy and excitement in your life.

A cat makes a leap of faith always sure that it will land on its feet. Have you ever seen a cat skeleton in a tree? We use that expression to describe someone who has succeeded on some life project; we say "he landed on his feet." You will never do anything exciting with your life unless you take leaps of faith. If the result is failure, isn't failure a greater teacher than success?

If your skin is dark, certain doors will not be open to you and you are not entitled to success in life. In many other countries and in some parts of this country this is true, where subtle shades of dark almost dictate your social status. What makes our country different is that we have laws and rules supporting your success. Many more doors have been forced open by this legislation. True, you will have to fight harder, but you can focus on any career and get there.

Some people are born losers and spend their lives getting out of difficult predicaments. Losers are not born, they're made! Victimization is the key word here. Unfortunately, our society today devotes more energy searching for scapegoats for its failures and disappointments, rather than taking responsibility for them and correcting and reversing them. The media reinforces this perception and offers choices of scapegoats. One of the messages, for example, is from the drug manufacturers who say staying well is now in their hands and that no matter what's wrong with you, don't try to heal yourself. Just take this latest miracle drug, even though it has a variety of possible negative side effects. If those side effects make you ill, there are other drugs to treat those side effects. As a last resort you can always find a lawyer eager to bring on a lawsuit for you.

Now what do you do to get out of this trap? Recognize that whatever situation you are in, negative or positive, you are there because you put yourself there. It is nobody's fault but your own and you have the power to move out of it—a power that you have never recognized before. This is a power you can now manifest to improve your life. If the same negative situations happen to you over and over, you now have the power to get out of the "revolving door." As you make this power work for you, your self-esteem grows. And as our self-esteem grows, we can learn to say no more often without feeling guilty. The approval of others becomes less important.

I am reminded of a client who had breast cancer. She and her husband were living in her in-laws' home in an Italian neighborhood. She and her husband, her in-laws, the unmarried aunt, a recently immigrated uncle, her husband's sister and her husband, all lived in this two-family house.

She was the only non-Italian in the family. They had been opposed to her marriage from the beginning and constantly reminded her that she was not one of them. They asked her what was wrong with her that she was not pregnant by now. The cruelest behavior of all was when they would all start speaking in their Italian dialect in her presence, laughing a lot, which made her feel that they were talking about her.

Her situation was so stressful that whatever good her chemotherapy was doing, it was being negated by her home situation. After a couple of sessions with me, she recognized that she had the power to move out. She moved in with a friend and in six months she was in remission.

A single parent cannot have a career and still be a good parent. This is another common perception which traps single mothers or fathers.

If you are a single mother, you may feel trapped and need contact with people. Go to work, even if you only have a part-time job which just covers the cost of day care. You will feel more fulfilled and less frustrated. A happy mother does a better job of parenting. Of course, there are exceptions as some mothers feel fulfilled staying at home and devoting all their energy to parenting. If you are a single father, you probably have a full-time job which meets your socialization needs.

A parent that was abused as a child will become an abusive parent. This is one of those "truths" promoted by psychiatrists and therapists. Because of the pain you suffered as a child, you decide to be a gentle parent, capable of tenderness combined with discipline. There are many cases such as these, where the children grow up not fearing their parents' wrath, but still respecting their wisdom in making decisions. This "truth" gives an abusive parent an excuse for being abusive. Another out would be to blame it on genetics.

If we wish to be perceived as a good person, we need to be willing to sacrifice ourselves to help others. To put ourselves first is selfish. Here we have a problem in defining a good person. Do we mean a person who is compassionate, able to really listen without appearing distracted, able to give without expecting thanks, who is loyal and dependable?

Sounds like a person who has completed the process offered in this book! This kind of person is often called self-actualized.

Becoming your own first priority does not make you a "bad" person. The word "selfish" is not such a negative word. The first requisite for being a good lover or partner is being in love with yourself. Thus you come into the friendship feeling whole and not dependent on your partner to boost a fragile self-esteem or meet emotional needs that you have not dealt with. Another bonus is that you discover the therapeutic benefits of being able to say no without feeling guilty or angry.

Pulling up stakes and moving to another state makes it easier to start a "new life." When you move to another state, you take your "baggage" (problems) with you. The stress of moving, adapting to a new environment and possibly a new job, may temporarily hide the problem areas in your life, but they will still need to be dealt with eventually. How much wiser to get these problems out of the way before leaving, which assures the beginning of a new and exciting life when you arrive at your new home.

I had a client—who had been through two wives—who decided to move to Vermont because he loved skiing. With the fresh air and the simple life he thought all his problems would go away. I heard from him from time to time, telling me of his most recent failed relationship. Several years later I received a very up and positive note from him saying that he had just completed a ten-week course at a wonderful drug and alcohol rehab center which had helped him acknowledge that for years he had been a secret alcoholic—secret in that he had hidden his alcoholism from himself and others in his life.

Having lots of money brings happiness and security into our lives. Thousands of Americans are driving themselves to making more and more money, and with it are buying million-dollar homes, vacation homes, yachts and speedboats (the faster the better), expensive luxury cars, extra large SUVs, pickup trucks and Hummers to feel powerful. As I write this, there is a new commercial showing a young man, who has just paid for a shopping cart full of meat, getting into his Hummer and charging forward. The sign under the image says "RESTORE YOUR MANHOOD." Do drivers of Hummers, Ford Expeditions and Mercedes look any happier than drivers of ordinary cars? Take a look the next time one passes you by. If you have your million-dollar house full of expensive TVs, electronic equipment, furs and jewelry, then security is assured only with elaborate and expensive alarm systems for your home, cars, boats and vacation homes.

Happiness is not for sale.

On *The New York Times* best seller list is a book that has been listed for several years called *Rich Dad Poor Dad*, which is about "teaching one's children how to get rich and stay rich."

If you want to be happy and stay happy, be needed! Be needed not only by family members or friends, but by some complete strangers that you may never meet. Do volunteer work for some charity or nonprofit group whose work you admire. You will feel a happiness that money cannot buy. The rich are so busy making money that they don't have time for volunteer work, so they write a check.

One of the side benefits of volunteer work is that it may identify a new career direction for you. If the nonprofit organization appreciates your work, they may offer you a full-time job or put you in touch with other organizations that have a job opening. Being needed also gives a great boost to your self-esteem.

In this section I have tried to challenge the most typical false perceptions. There are others, of course, which are not included. If you hold onto others, challenge them yourself.

CELL BAR THREE
Emotions and Feelings

Negative feelings such as guilt, fear, anger and pain can dominate our lives. It's almost as if a feeling—anger, for example—continually sits on our shoulders, popping up in situations when it is most inappropriate. As if ever present guilt drives us to buy gifts for friends and expect expressions of gratitude. We are driven to take over and carry out personal tasks for people who haven't asked for help. When we have to make a decision involving some kind of change or trying something new, fear dominates and we turn down opportunities for personal growth. When everyone around us is laughing exuberantly at some situation or joke, we find it difficult to give over to the spirit because of a chronic feeling of pain.

The process of clearing the energy invested in these negative feelings may take some time, but every time you work through the following exercise you will feel lighter and more free.

A first step is to recognize that these negative feelings are not all negative. We were given these feelings for our survival, without them we couldn't live for very long. It is only when they are present in such an intensity that they affect our judgment, and then they become truly negative. As an example, if we didn't feel fear before crossing the street, we might never make it to the other side. Anger produces the adrenalin rush that makes it possible to defend ourselves. Pain helps us to empathize with others' pain. Guilt may save an important relationship by compelling us to apologize for a hurtful behavior.

Where do these feelings come from? They come from our Long-Term Memory Bank which sits in the unconscious or Right Brain. This storage house has a record of all the events which have taken place in our life up until today. Our past emotional experiences, which have not been resolved, are implanted there. By unresolved I mean that the emotion generated has not been released. Imagine that you had a violent argument with your father and felt very threatened by his demands. Before you are allowed to present your position and release some of your anger, he walks out, refusing to continue the discussion. That event is filed in the Memory Bank, along with a whole lot of the energy of anger. If this encounter is repeated many times over the years, it builds a kind of pressure which will make itself felt just below the level of consciousness.

Here is the moment to practice Creative Visualization. (See the appendix on the principle and process.) Creative

Visualization is consciously creating a fantasy or image and transferring it into the unconscious or Right Brain by reliving a series of recent events in which anger was expressed, but not resolved and, with eyes closed, recalling the event. Now the difference here is that you imagine saying to your opponent that, instead of raging, you would like an appointment for later when you have calmed down and are able to resolve the conflict peacefully. Start your exercise by recalling the last time you were angry. This time fantasize resolving the conflict peacefully. Work your way back in time, knowing that every time you are resolving issues nonviolently you are reducing the pressure from the unconscious. If you have identified your dominating negative or negatives, work it through in the same way. Remember to begin with the most recent event and work your way backwards in time.

To be really effective, it is best to sit quietly, breathing slowly and deeply for at least ten minutes. Better still, meditate for ten minutes before creating your fantasy. Your Long-Term Memory Bank will then be more accessible.

CELL BAR FOUR
Lack of Choices and Options

We feel trapped in a miserable state of mind; we feel helpless and without any exits. No choices and no options appear. In times like these we feel sorry for ourselves, isolated and desperately lonely. There are always options. Even when we decide to throw in the towel and do away with ourselves, there are always other options.

Over the years I have infrequently, fortunately, received desperate phone calls from clients announcing that they were going to kill themselves. This is their last appeal for recognition. Unfortunately, it does not allow for dialogue. My response has been untypical. I don't beg them not to, but agree with them that they have the right to take their lives. But I ask them to do themselves a favor before killing themselves. Take paper and pencil and spend some time reflecting. Then make a list of choices available to them other than suicide and to please call me back when the list is finished. They usually call back in an hour and say that I have saved their life.

So if you are on your Pity Potty, get off it and make your list. Jot down whatever comes to mind without judging it for being possible or logical. Later as you review your list, you may find that the option you thought impossible might be the one you choose.

CELL BAR FIVE
Relationships and Friendships

Relationships and friendships, especially with negative people, make the escape particularly difficult. This is always true when substance abuse is involved. The role of the "enabler" is easier to play than to confront the addiction. Persons can remain trapped in these unhealthy relationships with addicted personalities for years and cannot see a way out. Joining an Al-Anon group can be a great help.

Negative friends can be like energy "vampires" and leave their positive friends wiped out after a visit. Their negative energy can be so destructive that after leaving a room full of friends, the friends remain stunned and in silence until they can recover.

Relationships with parents can also block growth. Parents have a hard time changing roles when their children become adults. To give up control and love their children unconditionally is a big step. It may need a period of separation before they are willing to negotiate a peaceful friendship with their children. Their absence is necessary for your freedom. As painful as it may be for you, you will have to let them go for a while.

One spring I offered a course in a retirement home. The course was called "Energy for Living." In addition to classes on nutrition, tips on better sleeping and journal keeping, we offered a session on how to negotiate a new relationship with your children. During role playing, one elderly lady imagined she was making a phone call to her daughter whom she hadn't seen for several years. She held the disconnected phone to her mouth and offered the most tender words of reconciliation that no daughter could possibly reject. Most of the other twelve participants were in tears when she finished.

This is a biggie! Your cellmate may be what is holding you back and the thought of leaving him or her is scary. At first, you decide to move on your own and somehow maintain a strong relationship with your partner. You hope that he or she will see the progress you are making and will want to join you. This is one fantasy that is not very likely to be fulfilled. In spite of your efforts to keep things the same, your partner may begin to feel rejected and isolated. This may be the needed force to move him or her forward. In any case, your choice remains to be locked in a negative relationship or become your own first priority and continue. The latter is the only positive choice.

If you have children, they will be supportive because as

you progress you become a better parent, less distracted and able to give them more attention and love.

If you work full time, then you spend more time on the job than at home. Be prepared to change jobs as part of your escape. You will have to seek employment elsewhere. Here is an opportunity to apply the technique of Creative Visualization.

Some years ago a client used the technique. He was having great difficulty with a boss who did not understand the highly technical work he was doing and constantly leaned over his shoulder asking questions and making useless suggestions. This was creating a great deal of stress for my client. Then we decided to apply Creative Visualization and "create" a new job for his boss that would keep him out of the office all day. It was important that the new job should be perceived as a promotion. He was to be appointed an inspector of educational and training programs for the whole state, which would require him to be on the road most of the time. My client created a visualization of him visiting a branch office and reviewing the training program with the local team leader. My client used the visualization each day in his meditation and on his long drive to work. Four months later the new job was created by top management and his boss "hit the road."

EXERCISE

Here is an exercise that will help you to better understand yourself and build a basis for your new lifestyle. Take a sheet of paper or use two facing pages in your journal and draw four columns. The one on the far left should be wide and the others just wide enough for writing a check mark. On the top of each of the right-hand columns, write the following words: Mine, Parents and Peers. Begin by writing a value in the left column and then make a check mark in one of the right-hand columns of the source of the value. An example might be: A wife needs to give up her job if it interferes with her husband's career. The source of this value might be "Parents." So make a check mark in the Parents column. Keep up the exercise until you run out of values and perceptions. Review your page and decide what values and perceptions are worth keeping in your new life and those you wish to reject.

CHAPTER

2

LETTING GO

The last chapter was full of vital information. Let's outline the points made before moving into this chapter.

- Cells have many bars, but they can all be removed.

- As in any planned jail escape, each step must be carefully reviewed and rehearsed before taking "the leap of faith."

- Some values and perceptions keep us in jail, but by rejecting them we are then free to leave.

- Some of our parents' values are still useful, while some of our peers' are not, and vice versa.

- A robust self-esteem is very helpful in this process.

- We need to be our own first priority.

- Take the time to acknowledge our achievements as they occur.

- Though we try to take our cellmate with us, he or she may not be ready to take a "leap of faith" and must be left behind.

- After a soft landing, we discover a wide range of options.

Now on to "Letting Go." This is a phrase that one hears a great deal, and it has become sort of a cliché. Some who use it are not quite sure what it means, but know it has something to do with relaxation and feeling free. As there are many opportunities for letting go, we have devoted most of this chapter to the process.

We need to let go of trying to control people and events that are not within our control. Placing expectations on others is not likely to succeed and will leave us with feelings of betrayal and a load of stress. The only person we need to control is us, and if done efficiently it can keep us busy.

Letting go of unreasonable expectations of ourselves is important. We recognize our limitations while setting goals. However, setting goals just a bit beyond our limitations adds spice to our lives.

Leaving the radio weather report on all day is not going to guarantee a fine day for your garden party. Recognize that you are not in control of the weather. Your energy will be best spent making alternative plans.

Letting go of accumulated junk, such as old mail, no longer useful records, magazines and newspapers, and empty boxes and containers is difficult and sometimes painful; but the sense of freedom once the process is over is a wonderful new experience.

Forgiving is part of letting go of resentment and the need for vengeance. The need to "get even" can be an obsession that takes over our lives.

If you can do all this, you will be mentally, spiritually and physically healthier. The energy released from negative feelings can now be applied to achieving positive goals.

VALUES

At the end of the last chapter you had an exercise on values. You were asked to review the list of values and eliminate those which are no longer useful to you. You have had time between chapters to rethink the process. As your new values will be the basis upon which your new life is designed, it is worth doing more work on it.

An example of your parents' generation's value might be that a child born out of wedlock has little hope for a great future and that single mothers need a man around the house. If you are a woman reader, you may decide at some stage of your life to have a child without getting married. Today, many women make this decision as they approach the age when they can no longer safely bring a child into the world. More and more single men are adopting children and becoming single fathers. In your parents' day such a possibility was unthinkable.

Your peers may believe that an open marriage with multiple sex partners responds honestly to peoples' real needs and guarantees a long-term marriage. Probably a minority of couples consider this an option.

You may wish to reject these values and create substitutes for your life. You may decide that in your new life an emotional and spiritual harmony will be the first priority in a relationship, rather than sexual compatibility which can come later on.

FRIENDS AND PARTNERS

If after some serious reflection you decide that your partner is holding you back, you then have to take the painful step of breaking up. It is worth trying to explain the changes that you have decided to make in your life, which your partner may not understand. You can say that you seem to have grown apart, which your partner certainly must have been aware of. If you do break up, wait at least six months before getting into another serious relationship. A one-year delay is even better. A good reason for the delay is that after some months you may discover that your new partner was meeting certain emotional needs that you no longer have. With your next partner you hope to create a healthy interdependency rather than a limiting dependency.

One of your past emotional needs might be sympathy for the pain of divorce.

Negative friends are also difficult to get rid of. They have developed a need for doses of your positive energy and are frightened by your withdrawal. You may be their only source of positive energy. Every time they call to invite you or make a date to go out together, you "sadly" regret that you are busy. Eventually they will stop calling. Perhaps they have found another positive energy source to tap.

CHOOSING A NEW LIFESTYLE

What kind of person are you? How would you like others to see you? We are not talking about faking it, but by becoming the person you really are—not the person who was in jail fantasizing a new life.

What about changing your appearance—cutting your hair short, growing a beard or mustache, losing weight or exercising to tone your muscles? Are you going to be more concerned about your physical health? Will your wardrobe be more trendy?

Will you trade in your station wagon for a red convertible or BMW sedan? As superficial as these changes may sound, they will have an influence on how you feel about yourself, although they will not necessarily make you happier.

What kind of social group would you like to be part of? What kind of friends would you like to have—artists, successful young people, more mature people in education or sports? Would you like to go to museums and art shows, "in" bars and lectures or sporting events? Would you like to join clubs for recreation and meet new people?

Are the responsibilities of your job utilizing all your talents? Have you reached a dead end with little possibility for promotion? Are you feeling passionate about your work? Can you take some courses and change the direction of your career? Do you need to write a new resume and look for another job?

Speaking of passion, what are you passionate about? What turns you on? Since you are changing jobs, apply for one that you believe you can be passionate about.

SPIRITUAL GROWTH

Set aside at least half an hour a day for nurturing your spiritual side. Take up meditation or yoga, and keep your journal up to date. If you decide not to meditate, at least sit in silence, breathing deeply for twenty minutes a day. These will do wonders for your immune system, allowing it to devote much more energy to keeping you healthy.

EXERCISE

Before moving on to the next chapter, please do the following exercise. Draw up a life plan based on the above steps and more if they come to you. Then write it up in your journal.

CHAPTER

3

MOVING ON

What are the two main obstacles to change? Impatience is the first and fear is the second. Most of the time, patience is a lesson for all of us to work on. We are programmed to want a "quick fix" for all problems. The discovery of the miracle of antibiotics, which made it possible to cure an illness in twenty-four hours, contributed to the expectation that problems could be solved overnight. We're a society on the move but sometimes do not know where we are moving to. We are so impatient that we typically do not take the time to figure where we want to go. Impatience just adds to the stress levels. We tend to be just as impatient with ourselves as with others. If we truly want to move on and liberate ourselves, then learning patience must be our first lesson.

There are many subtle ways in which fear inhibits change. Giving up the known for the unknown future is fearful. This fear is a common obstacle. Moving on calls for taking a big risk and trusting that the new situation will be less painful than the status quo. Another fear is that we are moving too fast and will make blunders along the way, so we hold back. We need to be patient but still move forward at a reasonable pace. The answer is to seek the pace that is comfortable for us. There is no time frame to satisfy. It took us many years to get where we are and it may take a few years to reach our goal of liberation. It is encouraging to know that healing usually takes less time than the time to get sick.

One successful way of reducing our fear, which is preventing us from moving on, is to create a supportive mini-community by inviting a couple of good friends to join us on our voyage. The chances are that some of our friends also feel imprisoned and would welcome the opportunity of joining us in our program. The purpose of a support group is to encourage us to take risks and have confidence in ourselves. If we don't always succeed, the group will help us to understand the message of the experience.

STOP FOR A MINI-ASSIGNMENT. Create what I call a refrigerator "Mantra." On a piece of cardboard or heavy paper, print in large letters the word "PATIENCE" and tape it to the refrigerator door. Every time you open the door you will be reminded. As your needs change, you can write a new card once in awhile. Although I believe "patience" will need to be there for a long time.

Another obstacle is the need for getting even or for vengeance against the person who is the bearer of misery in our life. This need can become an obsession and completely block our progress.

An example might be that if we have been living with an abusive person for a long time, we find that the satisfaction only comes from making them suffer in a retaliatory manner. Are we ready to move on and let them off easily? Holding this emotion becomes more harmful to us than to them. We are really not on this earth to punish people who have hurt us.

In a case where our partner is a substance abuser, we are often reluctant to give up the role of enabler. The enabler is the protector, denying that the person has an addictive problem and reassuring friends and family that everything is fine. This is a role that we can easily step into, particularly if we want our relationship to last. What keeps us going is the belief that some day the reassurances from the abuser will pay off and they will actually stop the addiction.

A few years ago a couple made an appointment for a joint consultation. Their marriage was on the rocks and their financial situation was precarious. Let's call him Horace and his wife Amber. Horace worked as a copywriter for a large ad agency in New York City. His daily commute lasted more than two hours, most of it on the commuter train ride. Amber worked for an agency which serviced rock groups and individual rock singers. In addition to accounting services, they offered booking and travel arrangements. Amber only had to spend one day a week in the city and worked the rest of the time at home. Their two children attended local schools.

Amber was concerned about Horace's frequent use of cocaine, although he always seemed normal at home. He didn't see his cocaine use as a problem, but as a means to enhance the quality of his work and stimulate his creativity. He was one of his agency's most productive copywriters and was given some of the agency's biggest and sometimes the most difficult-to-please clients. As the commuter train approached Grand Central Station, Horace went to the toilet and took his first snort of the day. Often during the day, particularly if he was scheduled to make a presentation to a potential client, he closed his office door and did another line.

Amber in her contacts with rock groups and singers witnessed a variety of drugs used by clients as casually as if they were smoking cigarettes. These drugs, according to them, enhanced their performance and gave them the energy to work long gigs. She realized that Horace was using cocaine for the same reasons and decided not to confront him. He was after all very sensitive. Things did not remain the same, as Horace increased his use and began using it on his return home at night, claiming it helped him to wind down after a particularly difficult day. Amber suggested he try marijuana to wind down instead.

Horace was buying more cocaine and paying higher prices. Amber, who paid the household bills by the tenth of each month, was shocked when the bank statement began to show large monthly cash withdrawals. When the bank loan officer called to ask why there had been no mortgage payment in three months, she decided to confront Horace as he had insisted from the beginning that he would make the payments with his salary.

Amber rehearsed her confrontation with him for the rest of the week, trying to release a sense of guilt she felt in confronting him. Finally on a Saturday morning while the children were doing their sports and with a quavering voice, she confronted him with her ultimatum. He had a choice, either sign up for a residential drug rehabilitation program or leave the house. Horace began to sob, begging Amber for her help in kicking his habit. How he needed her to help him. This response is typical of the addict's attempt to manipulate and buy more time.

This story does not have a happy ending for Horace who passed through two programs without successfully kicking his habit. He was not ready to leave his prison cell.

It has a happy ending for Amber who divorced Horace, sold the house and moved with her children to another state. She found a fulfilling job and began to find ways to make new and interesting friends. Amber's leap of faith had a soft landing!

Now let's get back to discussing the blocks to change.

We have a fear of failure, of making a mistake. We know from past experience that we gain more wisdom from reflecting on our failures than celebrating our successes. Do we really believe this or are we just parroting what we have heard? Celebrating successes is not to be shunned as it does build our self-esteem. Meditating on failure helps us to avoid making the same mistake again. It keeps us from getting stuck in a revolving door. Getting stuck in the revolving door is when we do not take the time to reflect on our failures and therefore have to face the same challenges more than once, until we learn the lesson. In our reflection on our failures, we ask ourselves what wrong choices did we make along the way. Were there any choices we did not see? Did we give ourselves enough time to make the wisest choices?

Can we now move on with confidence?

Your assignment was to draw up your plan and write it in your journal. What is the first change step you are going to make? Is it possible that you will fail? If you do, how will you deal with it? On the other hand there may not be a possibility of failure, as not all change has this potential. If you are anxious, choose as a first step one that is guaranteed to succeed. Keep in mind that no great steps are taken without our willingness to be vulnerable. It's a healthy self-esteem that helps us to heal the failure.

No relationship can be truly fulfilling without both parties taking risks and being willing to be hurt. If the first try does not work and we feel betrayed by ourselves or our partner, then we need to learn the most effective technique for us to heal our pain. We must take our time before trying again. In the last chapter I suggested waiting at least six months before working on a new relationship. We can make good use of the time by reflecting on how to meet our own needs without expecting our new partner to meet them for us.

Let's now address the changes you listed. Begin with physical changes as they are easier to make than emotional or spiritual ones—changing hairstyle, growing a beard (you can always shave it off, so no risk is involved), and choosing a new style of clothes, perhaps less dowdy and more youthful clothes of brighter and lighter colors. You always bragged that all you could do was boil water. What about taking cooking classes, as a future date might be impressed with your cooking abilities? Watching some whole makeover shows will give you some ideas. Buying a new car, racier and brighter in color, or buy a beige sedan if that suits you better.

You can make new, like-minded friends—as Amber learned—by joining groups, attending meetings open to the public or taking evening classes. Find a neighborhood gym and with the help of a trainer, design a personal exercise program. Consult a nutritionist and plan a healthy diet. A weight loss program can be part of this plan.

Don't forget to make your refrigerator mantra!

EXERCISE

The time has come to turn to the appendix on Creative Visualization techniques. Learn the method, believe in its power and see how to apply it to your program. We will wait for you at Chapter Four.

CHAPTER

4

THE PROBATION OFFICER

Welcome back! Join us as we move on.

As you progress on your voyage of mental and spiritual liberation, you will often feel lonely and begin to doubt whether you are making any forward movement. You question yourself, wondering if you are really ready to take the steps you have committed to. As I suggested in the last chapter, recruiting a companion or two to join you gives you greater confidence and support. In addition to these companions, you need a "Probation Officer" to keep you on the path. In theory, a Probation Officer has several roles: mentor, advisor, listener and authority figure. Unfortunately today's Probation Officer can only play the latter role because of huge caseloads. Your Probation Officer can assume all the positive roles with the exception of being an authority figure. Identify a person who appears to be already liberated and ask them to assume this role. As in the case of a correctional Probation Officer, you will report in about once a month. You will discuss your progress, setbacks and fears, and ask for support. Bring your journal with you to these meetings so that nothing of importance will be forgotten. Preparing notes in advance would also be helpful. So often after an important meeting we are discouraged to find that we have forgotten an important point we would like to have made. Good reason for making notes. It is preferable that this person not be your mate or spouse.

After setting up this support system, the next move is to clear your life of negative friends and people. They are not difficult to identify, like vampires they leave you feeling depleted and discouraged. These types are difficult to let go of. They are so needy that the more you withdraw, the more aggressive they become in demanding pieces of your time. They are like an inmate who shouts and rattles the cell bars, but really is not ready to be released and give up victimhood. Later I will offer some detaching techniques.

Letting these people go without feeling guilty is almost impossible. You feel that you are abandoning them. Remind yourself that not long ago you were in the same position. They are facing the same choices that you did.

Let's look at some of the classical negative types. What they have in common is that they sap your strength and leave you doubting the reality of your vision. Choosing feelings of guilt over your life's survival is not a viable choice.

One common type is the man or woman friend who uses up most of your time discussing his or her failing marriage. This repeated litany of complaints is always the same. After a while, in desperation, you suggest divorce as an option. Telling them what to do is least helpful and falls on deaf ears. This suggestion is barely acknowledged as your suggestions are not a part of their program, which is to endlessly seek support and sympathy. Isn't it true that often when people ask our advice it isn't that they intend to follow it, but it is for reinforcing what they have already decided to do. Be honest. Of all the advice we have received in our lifetime, how much of it have we followed? We begin as teenagers believing that we have all the answers we need. As parents or older friends, we want to protect them so we warn them of pitfalls. They don't follow our advice. Often in life, we have to go through a negative experience in order to learn the inherent lesson which cannot be learned from another's experience.

What about those friends who are chronically ill? It's almost as if they are enjoying their ill health. We forget and make the mistake of asking them how they are when we speak on the phone. We then receive a list of new ailments with accompanying, sometimes gruesome details, which makes for a colorful conversation. We are presented with images of deteriorating organs, hemorrhages, spasms and fainting spells. I don't wish to sound heartless here, but there are people who use illness for self-validation. There are other benefits to illness, and among them are evading responsibility by postponing important decisions, using sympathy for forgiveness, getting attention, avoiding jail (heart pains on the way to court), and punishing ourselves for a misdeed.

I was always in trouble in school and on the verge of being suspended, so I developed a skill for creating a timely bilious attack, accompanied by vomiting. This illness usually required a couple of days at home and allowed the school authorities to feel less inclined to suspend me after a few days. It did not seem right to punish a returning student who looked pale and sickly. This is a ruse I used for many years. It began by forcing myself to eat numbers of spoons of peanut butter in one afternoon. This usually brought on vomiting by evening. Later on I didn't need the peanut butter. (I hope that some of my old teachers don't read this book.)

Then there are the predictors of doom. No matter what we express as positive goals for the future, they immediately predict sure failure and disaster. If something positive happens to them, they refuse to acknowledge it. These persons want so badly to be right that they choose what they feel is the more likely outcome for their predictions, failure and even disaster.

Some friends discuss mutual friends critically and negatively, thus inviting us to become their loyal and steadfast friend. One wonders what they say about us in later conversations with mutual friends.

At times we find ourselves in a new situation among strangers. One person seems to seek us out and force a friendship on us.

I am reminded of a young MBA graduate from Harvard who set his job goals for employment at one of the most prestigious law firms in New York. He was successful and on his first day of work he was very nervous and anxious to please. The firm was full of apparently very motivated and aggressive corporate lawyers who, with the exception of one person in the office, ignored his presence. Several times during the day he felt this person's eyes on him. At the end of the day this person came over to his desk and suggested that they have a drink together. By the second drink our MBA graduate began to feel uncomfortable with his drinking companion, who became cloying and almost seductive in implying that they had become steadfast friends. He also recognized faces of some of his fellow employees lined along the bar. None greeted his new friend and when they looked his way, they appeared to feel sorry for him. It turned out that the companion was generally disliked and distrusted by his colleagues. It took some weeks before our MBA man was able to be accepted by others at the firm. The simple lesson here is to move slowly into a new position and check things out before accepting overtures. Every organization has needy people who take advantage of strangers to fulfill their needs.

Finally, there are friends who dominate the meeting by talking exclusively about themselves and the events in their lives. Perhaps at the end of our meeting they remember to ask how we are doing, but appear not to be listening to the answer as they take their leave. These persons usually complain that people are not friendly in their town and that where they came from the situation was different. Wherever they go they will have the same problem because they never show any real interest in our affairs unless they can relate it to theirs. They are called "solipsists."

I am sure that you can add to this list from personal experience.

Now what is the most polite way to drop these negative and destructive people? Here are a few suggestions. If these friends are polite, they will call you in advance of their visit. You can say that you are sorry a visit is not right at this time as you are very busy or you might make the conversation brief by saying that you are entertaining a visitor. If they arrive unannounced, as soon as they arrive suggest that they always call before coming as your life is very busy. Then start looking for your car keys, saying that you don't want to be late for an appointment. Another ploy is to refuse to hug them or touch their hands by saying you are suffering from some new virus and you don't want them to catch it. Or that the visit must be very brief as you are expecting an important long distance business call in five minutes. Little white lies are okay if they are made to protect peoples' feelings. Some sample replies might be, "I'd love to, but I can't…" or "I'm really sorry, but I can't…."

If as a reader of this manual you wish to visit me, call ahead and I won't pull any of these tricks, but will tell you when I am free to meet with you.

Guard your positive friendships as they can reinforce your personal commitment and support your self-esteem. They will also encourage you to take responsibility for your actions. Their love is mostly unconditional and with a positive attitude, they can make your future seem bright.

Negative experiences and locations can also sap your positive energy. Become sensitized to negative energy fields and trust your "gut" feelings. Your "gut" feelings are messages from your Higher Self, and in this case are warnings. I am not proposing that you become totally paranoid, but today we are assaulted by so much negativity that we cannot control that a little paranoia helps to maintain our positive energy field.

Here's an example. Suppose that a friend invites you to go to the movies and you have seen previews and it appears to have a lot of violence in it. Decline the invitation. A weekend of television can be very destructive. Local and world news broadcasts, special reports on the latest disaster can drag on for days, and sitcoms of police and crime shows and emergency room hospital shows together can wipe out a week's good work.

Try this experiment. Decide not to watch television for a weekend. Refrain from watching any news broadcasts and weather reports. (I believe that weather people are closet sadists and seem to enjoy creating panic among their viewers.) Forecasters seem dedicated to raising your stress levels by predicting invisible patches of black ice on the roads, dangerous commutes, power outages and school closings. And in spite of their highly developed radar systems, they are only correct in their predictions about eighty percent of the time. (The nineteenth-century farmer who sucked on his finger and raised it in the air could predict quite accurately the following day's weather.) On Monday morning you'll feel more ready to face the week ahead. Someday there will be a popular restaurant called TGIM (Thank god it's Monday). I am a true optimist.

There are certain retail establishments that show little interest in serving their customers. One feels unwelcome. We hesitate to ask for information or some unusual product. If they don't carry it, they seldom offer to order it for you and sometimes they say, "That product is no longer available." You usually find it at the next store you try. Those establishments should not be in the retail business. They eventually fail, wondering why. Most clients who have similar experiences go to their competitor in the future. Find a store with more cheerful staff.

Here again, be sensitized to energies and if you feel discomfort in a supermarket, find another. Instead of shopping in a local one, I drive an extra five miles to shop in a supermarket that makes me feel comfortable.

Some streets and neighborhoods make one uncomfortable. Avoid them and find alternate routes. Super highways tend to be heavy with traffic, particularly in summer time. A cloud of anger energy hangs over the frustrated drivers. It is a very unhealthy place to be. In addition, the fumes of overheated engines are not good to breathe. Follow the back roads, they will take less time and the scenery is more interesting.

EXERCISE

On two opposite pages, write the following: on the left page write what you believe are your negative qualities and on the right, list your positive ones. The left page usually ends shorter than the right. If it isn't, work some more on the right. Be fair to yourself.

CHAPTER 5

LOVE THYSELF

The time has come to build up your self-esteem. As you make discoveries that are negative in your search of past events, your self-esteem is being tested more and more. Your level of self-esteem is like a savings account which you draw upon from time to time. Somewhere along the line you need to make some deposits to cover your withdrawals. How about firing up a love affair with yourself? Use some of the suggestions in the following paragraphs to lift your spirits.

Self-esteem is like blood pressure. It is never a constant and keeps going up and down depending upon recent events and current situations. When it is strong enough to allow you to take risks fearlessly, then you know that you have done your homework. When you can face challenges with your head up and shoulders braced, go for it!

Keep feeding it positive messages by acknowledging

small accomplishments, no matter how trivial you may feel they are. Some examples might include: paying your bills on time, answering a letter that has been lying around for a long time, fixing a toaster cord, making a presentation at a Rotary luncheon, donating food to the local food bank and apologizing for being thoughtless or even offensive in remarks. All these acts are worthy of acknowledgment. It helps to take some time, possibly during meditation, to review these events.

Check yourself on the words you typically use when referring to your abilities or in making a commitment to carry out an assignment. Do you frequently use "maybe I can," "perhaps," "I'll try," "fat chance" or "forget it"? When you drop something or break a glass, do you call yourself a "clumsy jerk" or "stupid ———"? Forgive yourself and get a dustpan and brush, reminding yourself that you still have five glasses. If you drop a roll on the floor, once you have seen the condition of the floor, you may decide to sweep the kitchen and throw the roll out for the birds.

Acknowledge your capabilities, as well as your limitations. When you set goals for yourself, set them just a bit beyond limitations. This small risk adds spice to your life, bringing an extra surge of adrenalin and a few minutes of a faster heartbeat. If you succeed in achieving the goal, then you really have something to congratulate yourself for. Thousands of roller coasters around the country offer "thrills" which create an adrenalin surge and rapid heartbeat. An alien looking on would wonder why earth people risk their lives on these rides and pay for it besides.

When George was in the final semester of his second year at college, his father had a massive stroke that left him totally paralyzed and unable to work. He was no longer able to pay George's college fees. George dropped out of college and came home. He got a job in a factory which made medical appliances. His mother felt that since he was unable to get a college degree, his future was limited and a professional career was not an option for him.

Because of his intelligence and ability to communicate well, he was soon promoted to shop boss. As a shop boss he was appreciated by his subordinates, as well as the executives of the company. However, it soon became clear to him that a promotion to a salaried executive position was not in his future, so he decided to look for other work.

On Sunday afternoons he would search the help wanted ads looking for an opportunity with a brighter future. One Sunday a large display ad appeared that caught his attention. A well known manufacturer of small kitchen appliances was announcing its expansion into new territories. The ad listed desirable qualities, including self-starter, personable, outgoing and finally, with a college education. The ad also mentioned that there were advancement opportunities. He felt that he met all the qualities except a college-level education. Because he had been to college, he felt that he had a college level of intelligence. The ad probably listed a college education as a means of sifting out unqualified candidates, so he decided to phone for an interview.

He had a job search manual at home which suggested that gathering as much information about the company would make him more impressive as a candidate. He spent the next three nights at the local library gathering information about the company from various directories, including the names of the top executives, annual sales and credit rating.

The Wall Street Journal had an article announcing the

company's new product: a rotisserie/convection oven which it was promoting nationwide. On the way home he stopped at an appliance store to see the oven and ask the salesman a number of questions about sales and typical customer reactions.

The job search manual also stated that it was important to take charge of the interview from the beginning. One tip was not to sit down until asked by the interviewer. This was a way of getting the interviewer's full attention and forcing him or her to put other work aside.

He opened the interview by discussing what he had learned about the company, not about himself. He mentioned his visit to the appliance store and reported on the conversation he had with the salesman. It became clear to him that he was now in charge of the interview, as the interviewer looked stunned and at the same time impressed. When finally the interviewer asked George about previous sales experience, George evaded the answer by describing his present employment and his success as a shop supervisor and how, with his communication skills, he had been able to improve employee attitudes about management. It had become clear that because of the small size of the company he would have to move on if he wanted to advance himself. The interviewer then asked George about his family background, if his parents were alive and did he have siblings. Then George took over again and began a discussion of today's economy and the pros and cons of Globalization. He then said that he was willing to start at a low level, providing there was the potential for climbing up the company structure.

The interviewer called his secretary and asked her to get Mr. Ball on the phone. Because of his research, George recognized the name of the vice president in charge of sales.

"Harry, I have an impressive young man in my office that I think you should meet."

Mr. Ball was welcoming and asked them to sit at his conference table. The interviewer gave a brief rundown on the interview. Mr. Ball then asked George about his availability and family needs. When George said that he wasn't married, he became more attractive as a candidate.

Mr. Ball said, "He looks good to me. Make him an offer and let me know the follow up. Thanks, Bill."

The interviewer gave George his direct line number and an application form. He suggested that George call at the end of the week, as there were several candidates being interviewed for sales positions over the next few days.

George was hired and is now assistant sales director for the Northeast Region. George's experience sends us several messages. In every job interview there is a risk of being rejected, even if we meet all the criteria. If we want the interview to go our way, we just don't sit meekly waiting for the first question. By opening the interview, we give the interviewer a needed break. He or she has probably been through several interviews already and had to work hard to ask all the questions of less outgoing candidates. We can also say that George set his goal beyond his limitations and the risk involved set into motion an adrenalin charge (I called it spice earlier), which gave him more confidence.

There was a time in my checkered career when I designed and ran a job search workshop for recently released prison inmates. Talk about limitations!

The following suggestions were presented at the first session: enter the room with your head up and with a slight smile on your face, do not sit down until asked to do so, sit up straight and look the interviewer in the eyes. Don't begin by saying "I need a job." Of course you do; otherwise you wouldn't be there. Ask what the company's needs are and what skills they are looking for. Make an opportunity to tell the interviewer what you believe are your positive qualities. Talk in generalities about pre-jail experiences. If you have a wife and children, tell the interviewer as that tends to make you seem more responsible. Now is the time to let the interviewer take over. If he or she appears interested, openly mention that you have just been released from jail and DON'T say that you were innocent and wrongly jailed.

Except for the final session, all others involved the ex-offenders' role-playing interviews. After learning some of the principles of ideal behavior, they critiqued each other. Learning how to walk and enter the interviewer's office, how to sit, how to look at the interviewer, what to wear and to speak clearly were all included in the lesson. They learned how to reveal the recent incarceration in the least threatening manner, as well as answering the questions about the incarceration clearly.

I am wondering why I included this information here. It may be helpful to some readers who plan a new job as part of their new life. It is possible that some readers have actually been incarcerated and will find this useful.

Another self-esteem related issue is a fear of success. To those who haven't experienced it, it sounds ridiculous; but for others it is a recurring life problem. Since the reasons for self-destructive behavior are hidden in events of early life, it requires some extensive work and some therapy sessions to challenge. It does require that the person who suffers from it must first acknowledge that it has been a problem in their lives. In life we set specific goals, devote great energy to their achievement, and just before their completion, we sabotage them. Some of the more obvious examples might include the college students who drop out in the last semester of their senior year; the employee who on the eve of a job promotion interview gets "tanked" and arrives at work the next day hung over and bleary eyed; the bride who believes herself unworthy of happiness and disappears on the eve of her marriage; and finally, the artist who begins what will turn out to be his or her best canvas, but doesn't finish it, leaving it stacked in a storage room for years.

Clinical studies have found that the problem often begins with early childhood experiences. Sometimes it is connected to a child's school performance. Often the parents are highly motivated and lead very stressed lives. They are not satisfied with their child's average class standing and unhappy with report cards showing low or average marks. The child dreads bringing home a "bad" report card, and in some cases tells the parents that the card was lost on the school bus, hoping that the parents will not call the school for a copy. Even though the parents appear to love them as always, the child fears the loss of love and feels guilty and unworthy. This process of turning the guilt into a low self-esteem is buried in the Long-Term Memory.

Another more obvious cause for the fear of success is that success calls for new responsibilities and changes which the person may not wish to commit to. It is easier to slip into invisibility as a failure—joke about being lazy—than stand up and be counted.

One of the most debilitating habits, partially related to the fear of success, is what I call "rehearsing." Rehearsing is a mental spiral that whirls endlessly, particularly when we lie in bed unable to sleep. The mind fantasizes on past negative experiences or creates a long list of "what ifs" in a planned future event. Often the past experiences were humiliating and showed one's inadequacy in dealing with the challenge. The "what ifs" express fear of not handling the future situation to one's advantage. If we have to defend ourselves, will we come out unscathed? If when we wake up in the middle of the night with a new pain, we fantasize going to the doctor who with solemn face tells us that it sounds to him like the beginning of cancer. The next vision may be of us being wheeled into the operating room.

What do you need to do to get off this merry-go-round? If you are sleeping alone, say out loud in a clear voice, "STOP REHEARSING." If this does not work, get out of bed and walk around, even go to the kitchen and have some ice cream or something comfortingly sweet. When you return to bed, lie down on the opposite side and begin by counting your breaths. Soon, strange and weird images begin to appear, one on top of each other. This is a sign that you are back to sleep.

Remembering past humiliations, betrayals and what you perceive as defeats, act as setbacks to your program for building your self-esteem. Another negative effect of fantasizing future challenges as being doomed to fail, they become self-fulfilling prophecy. Approach the future challenge with the spirit of a winner. Remember George who went to his interview with the visualization that he would get the job.

As I mentioned earlier, there is an exercise of rehearsal that is positive and healing; in this case reliving a past experience that has generated a negative feeling and then rescripting it into a positive experience, thus cleansing it of the feeling. This can release chronic feelings of pain, fear, guilt and anger which are sitting in your Long-Term Memory and causing internal stress in your life. You will better understand the process by doing the exercise.

As in all exercises for healing the Right Brain Long-Term Memory, it is important to begin with a period of meditation or deep and slow breathing for at least ten minutes. Your breath intake must begin by expanding or pushing out your stomach, followed by filling your lungs. This forces the diaphragm to participate in the breathing and opens up the lower half of your lungs. Many of us have the tendency of shallow, more rapid breathing which leaves our lower lungs unused and often full of toxic gases. If you have decided to work on chronic feelings of fear, begin by looking upward with your eyes closed and seeing a blank screen. Now, with a magic marker which produces sparkling gold lines, slowly write the word "FEAR" on the screen. Gaze quietly at the word and try to remember events in your past that produced feelings of fear. Now remember the most recent fearful event. Rescript the event, but this time you demonstrate courage and ability to be in constant control of the situation. Enjoy the triumph and see yourself surrounded by an aura of gold light which feels secure and powerful. At your next exercise on fear, you need to go back to the event before the last and work it through. Work your way into your past as far back as you can remember. You are then ready to work on other chronic negative feelings using the same exercise. The benefits of these experiences leave a positive effect on your future life. If you have read the section on Creative Visualization, you will recognize this skill.

Over the months as you work deeper in your Memory Bank, you will begin to feel free of these negative feelings and respond less emotionally to situations.

Another useful suggestion is to generate positive feelings throughout your day. Try to see conflicts from both points of view, whether they are social or political. Remember "it takes two to tango."

As you go through the day, perhaps while commuting to work, review your attitudes and reactions to situations, particularly unexpected ones. If you can find time, review the day's events in the evening. With this retrospective process you will be able to set some goals for change.

EXERCISE

There are two sides to a coin: a positive and a negative one (heads and tails). In your journal, list the negative perceptions you have of happenings in your life. Then flip the coin and describe what might be the benefits of these experiences and lessons to be learned. Take time to reflect on them and you will never have to face the same challenges again. You may remember the "revolving door" mentioned earlier.

CHAPTER 6

WHO NEEDS EXPECTATIONS?

In a previous chapter I described the dangers of placing expectations on others and consequent feelings of betrayal when they fail to achieve them. In the last chapter we agreed that we need to set expectations for ourselves to achieve the goals of our program and other positive personal goals. We don't need to fulfill others' expectations unless we do so voluntarily.

Others' expectations tend to be misdirected and destructive. Remember in the last chapter that one of the causes of the fear of success was when parents put unrealistic school performance expectations on a child of average intelligence. Fathers who sign up a son for soccer team, whether the son wants to play or not, are disappointed when he doesn't score a goal or two. It happens sometimes that this father was a failure in sports at school and treats his disappointment by imposing stardom on his son. And when the son doesn't come home a hero, he feels guilty and unworthy of his father's love.

I am troubled when I read of parents forcing their very young children to read and write, when at their young age they should be developing social skills. The goal here is to push their children way ahead of their peers in school and thus give them an advantage of "beginning careers" at an early age. Can we assume that in adulthood they will be joyful and well adjusted?

Unrealistic expectations placed on us don't end with childhood. As adults we can invest a lot of energy in meeting others' expectations. During the struggle we lose sight of our vision and soon we don't know who the "real" me is. If we expend most of our energy pleasing others, there is no time left to please ourselves. Perhaps our life purpose is only to please others. Do you believe that Thomas Edison, Jonas Salk, Margaret Mead or Albert Einstein were driven by others' expectations? The visionaries and inventors of civilizations are dedicated to pleasing themselves in their work and then perhaps benefiting society. Most of these creators were perceived as antisocial oddballs.

So if we want to fight back when others place limits upon us, here's a silencer: "What you sees is what you gets." There is really no possible answer to that one.

As we noted earlier, we are often disappointed when placing expectations on others. If their spirit is in it, they are probably doing the best they can. Placing unreasonable expectations on a person with whom we have a close relationship is an invitation to friction and in some cases leads to divorce and separation. What do we mean by unreasonable here? Simply, if we expect that person to change to meet our standards and values. Believing that with an extra effort on our part they will change is a recipe for self-betrayal. Over time, and for a number of reasons, that partner may feel more secure and will voluntarily and unconsciously make positive changes that will surprise and please us. It is time to turn to our refrigerator mantra: PATIENCE.

If we have been in a long-term relationship which has been supported by each one looking to satisfy personal needs by placing responsibility on the partner, then the struggle for self-realization and independence is a tough one. To put it differently, we have the responsibility to sort out our own issues. This might be letting go of chronic negative feelings which I mentioned earlier or building up our self-esteem. By leaving our partner behind in prison, it means that we accept taking responsibility for making positive changes. The one left behind may not have recognized his or her own issues and becomes very anxious at facing things alone. The discovery that they are on their own, having to take full responsibility for themselves, can be frightening. Not everyone is ready to leave prison.

When we learn the technique of Creative Visualization and practice it, it may appear to contradict what we have been saying about the negative effect of creating expectations, particularly on other people. Not really, as most visualizations are not designed to change people but to create opportunities and circumstances that can be very helpful in our effort at creating a fulfilling life for ourselves. Finding the perfect job or career, the ideal home or partner, are just some of the goals we include. In the latter case we are not trying to change a person, but we are sending out an appeal for someone who meets our criteria. This turns out to be one of its most successful uses. If we create a visualization to change a boss or colleague whom we dislike, what happens is that they don't really change but gradually, if unconsciously, our perceptions of them modify as we begin to discover some of their positive characteristics, and we find that they don't get to us as much. Finding the perfect job or career using the technique is much easier.

Because of high nationwide unemployment figures at the time I offered a workshop called "Stuck," in order to qualify the participants had to have been looking for work for two or more years. After spending several sessions discussing the power of negative and positive energies and helping participants shed their defeatist attitudes, we moved on to the task of identifying desirable jobs, which often involved a change in career direction. Each one began by listing their natural skills and positive personality qualities that they would need to cite in an interview. After identifying the position, they researched the appropriate job description and educational requirements. This information was available on the internet and in local libraries and was part of an ongoing assignment.

As the weekly sessions continued, some participants went out on their own and applied for their preferred jobs, for which they were not really qualified. Because of the techniques they had learned for taking charge of the interview, their apparent passion and their emphasis on meeting the employer's needs, they were hired. I remember one in particular who applied for the job of social worker in a local city government, even though she had no experience. In her research she had found a job description for such a position and described what she felt might be some of her responsibilities in such a position. To her great excitement, she was hired. Here we need to remember George's experience and how he used the same techniques to be hired even though he had neither past job experience nor a college education. By the end of the workshop, most had found jobs or had promises of employment. The remainder did not find work for personal reasons, minimal financial pressure and, in some cases, low self-esteem. We have to be "gutsy" to take the risk of rejection and use this technique.

Because of the destructive effects on your life of trying to meet others' expectations, you need to do some more work on it. As you contemplate your life until now, you will discover how often you have pushed your needs aside in order to accommodate others. Once you acknowledge these, you will find it easier to reject them. This search of the past and even near present should continue from now on. Your long-term goal is to become your own first priority and care little about what people think of you. You will then experience inner peace.

EXERCISE

Actually this last suggestion of reviewing your past will be your exercise.

CHAPTER 7

MEET YOUR HIGHER SELF

There are many names given to this spiritual part of our brain which I believe is also our immortal self. Of course, there are "devout" atheists who do not believe in the soul or that there is an immortal part which remains intact after death. Other names given it include: inner voice, guardian angel, soul self and spiritual self. The atheists tend to call it "alter ego," once they acknowledge that mystical part of the brain. Whatever name we give it, it is a truly powerful part of us and without it we would not exist as human beings. (I wonder if a carrot has a soul.) Most of us only barely acknowledge its existence and have not discovered how we can consciously apply its wisdom in making important life decisions.

We who have decided to take this transformational voyage of prison escape could not have succeeded so far without the silent support of our Higher Self. If it had not approved of our decision, it would have showered us with negative intuitive messages. The person remaining in prison must have received such warnings. A hunch, a "gut feeling" or what sounds like an "ahaaa," usually comes from the Higher Self, particularly if we are dealing with a vital issue. For this reason we need to listen to and trust these messages as they surface and act upon them without reservation. We are brought up to believe that acting on hunches is dangerous and that the messages are not to be trusted, especially since they are seldom logical. Most of these cautions come from persons who are Left Brain dominant. The Right Brain-dominant person who receives them knows to trust them. If we modify their recommendations to make more sense and make them more "logical," they lose their effectiveness and can confuse the situation.

There are many examples in history of leaders in industry and the arts who never completed even a minimum level of education, but who demonstrated great achievements by depending only on their Higher Self's hunches. Great fortunes were made by eighth-grade graduates who made important strategy decisions on hunches.

As I write this manuscript, there is a book called *BLINK* which has been on *The New York Times* Best Seller List for weeks. The book's description in the reviews describes the message that hunches are to be trusted. The book gives several anecdotes showing that management decisions, made as a result of a hunch, have saved financial losses and embarrassment. I was disappointed in the book because it did little to imply the source of these hunches. I believe that its greatest contribution is that it legitimizes the hunch and its value as a part of any decision-making process, thus refuting a long-held prejudice.

The Higher Self skills in problem solving can save us hours of searching for a solution using our conscious and intellectual mind, which is limited by its expectations that the answers will be logical and reasonable. By presenting our problem to our Higher Self just before going to sleep and asking for a good solution to surface when we wake up, will involve precedent (Long-Term Memory) and wisdom (our Higher Self). The solution upon awakening is clearly the best possible solution we can expect. Our reaction to the exciting answer is "Why didn't I think of that!" Well we did, but not by using our conscious or Left Brain.

The Right Brain, also known as the unconscious, can be frivolous and misleading, whereas the Higher Self will always be dependable and wise. How can we identify the source? The first will be disconnected and interspersed with contradictions, whereas the second seriously describes a reasonable procedure. Its recommendations will always be in our best interest. Since the Higher Self sits on top of the Right Brain, it does not have the verbal skills of the Left Brain. Therefore its messages are often presented in image form. The difference is that, unlike bizarre dream images, its nonverbal message becomes clear after a brief consideration.

A reliable means to verbalize complicated messages from the Higher Self is to consult the *I-Ching*, an ancient Chinese oracle. Carl Jung, the psychiatrist with much more emphasis on the spiritual being than Freud, found it very helpful in his work with patients. I have used it for years as a means for affirming what a person has decided to do for themselves during our two sessions together. At the end of the second and last session, the client will toss three coins six times and the resulting hexagram (pattern) will choose one of 64 overviews that will verbally identify and support the program that the client has designed for the future. The person is always amazed at the appropriateness of the recommendations to their vision for the future. The literal translations of the *I-Ching* are very difficult to interpret. Those of us who use it frequently are grateful to the author R.L. Wing for his excellent interpretations in his *I-Ching Workbook*. His attempt to adapt the vocabulary and recommendations to modern culture has made the workbook very useful. In addition to consultation support, there is another use which can also be very helpful in future life planning and solving present life dilemmas. In this case, we write our specific question for advice. The question cannot require a yes or no answer, but can be in the style of asking for advice or a new perspective on a personal life situation. We find the advice very helpful in making choices. There is, however, a danger of creating a dependency on the *I-Ching* by constantly consulting it when faced with challenges which we could resolve easily by using our good sense. In such instances the Higher Self, understanding the importance of our need to take responsibility for our actions, will deliberately give us confusing and contradictory answers so that we give up the dependency. The *I-Ching* does not belong on your coffee table.

How do I get in touch with my Higher Self you ask? By being silent and peaceful. This is why you need to meditate daily. If you find it difficult to meditate, don't get stressed out about it. Just agree with yourself to sit in complete silence, no background music allowed, for twenty minutes to half an hour. As in meditation, you still breathe slowly and deeply to relax. Then with your eyes closed, send the message to your Higher Self that you are open to suggestions which often come in image form. Our next step is to interpret the meaning of the images, just as you would if you were interpreting dreams. Daily meditations or silent periods offer many benefits to your health. It allows your immune system to heal without having to cope with cleansing your body of adrenalin surges brought about by stressful situations. The silence also encourages the production of antibodies and other disease-fighting microorganisms. Soon you will feel more inner peace and more energy.

As you develop your own method for consulting your Higher Self, you can contact it with specific questions. In the area of wellness, since the Higher Self monitors all the happenings in your body, a question about your health is appropriate. If, for example, I have a sudden sharp pain which may persist for a few days, I ask my Higher Self whether I should be concerned. I act upon the answer and if the answer is no, I let it go. If the answer is yes, then I decide which health professional I will contact. This trust has developed over many years. Reading this book does not guarantee this kind of relationship for you and I urge you not to try it. For me it has worked and I enjoy remarkably good health. Perhaps some day you will feel comfortable with a similar relationship.

While experiencing a serious illness, the Higher Self can become an important partner in our recovery. Setting up a weekly meditation appointment with it, can keep us up to date on the progress we are making toward wellness. While recovering from emphysema, I would ask my Higher Self each week to present me with a "picture" of my lungs. If a black spot appeared on one of my lungs, I would concentrate on that spot during the following week. Usually the next week it would not appear in the "picture" and I felt reassured.

Listening to your Higher Self's hunches about people you meet for the first time or people with whom you are about to do business with will save you a lot of grief. Here again we are warned against judging people from first impressions. In almost all cases our Higher Self has been right. Somewhere down the line, when the contact becomes negative, we remember that first impression. As your relationship strengthens, you won't have to make a call to your Higher Self to receive advice; it is offered automatically when appropriate.

Finally, I believe that the Higher Self is involved in sending out requests in thought forms to fulfill Creative Visualizations. There is a level of spiritual communication between Higher Selves that we are not conscious of, but that goes on all the time. On this level there are no space or time limitations.

In the mid-fifties I witnessed a mind-blowing ESP (extra sensory perception) experiment in California. At the time, the only significant research in the fields of telepathy and psychic phenomena was being carried out by Dr. Rhine at Duke University.

For the first time, interest in these kinds of experiments was publicly acknowledged. The purpose of the California experiment was to prove that on this psychic level of communication there were no space or time limitations. A hypnotherapist from New Jersey, who was visiting friends in Southern California, was a member of an ESP study group which met on Sunday nights in Lincoln Park, New Jersey. Members of the group included scientists, doctors, teachers and others. Three hours earlier than the time of the Sunday meeting in New Jersey, the hypnotherapist placed a subject in California under a light trance, making it possible for him to speak, and asked that person to attend the New Jersey meeting and describe in detail what the participants looked like, including the clothes they were wearing. All the while she took notes. The subject also described that there was a rain shower taking place which the participants did not seem aware of. A few weeks later the hypnotherapist compared her notes with her New Jersey friends and confirmed every thing that her subject in California had recounted!

This account helps us to recognize how little we know about the functioning of the brain and that we must always remain "open minded" to new discoveries we save for those who are know-it-alls. They are found everywhere.

This experiment involved only a fraction of communication that is taking place above and around us all the time. If we could develop this skill, we would not need cell phones. The mother, who worries about her child who happens to be far away and checks daily on its well-being, uses another level of communication other than the cell phone. If the child becomes ill, the mother knows immediately. When you receive a phone call from the person you were just about to call, it is perhaps another level of communication. When you "send out" a description of the type of person you need to hire for a specific job and that person turns up looking for work in a couple of days, that's another communication level. A businessman I know staffs his business in this manner. We will discuss these forms more in the next chapter as we create some visualizations.

EXERCISE

Please reflect on important past life decisions and how they were made. Did you make them on a hunch or a "gut feeling"? (Maybe our Higher Self lives in our gut.) Write in your journal what you discover. You may have been benefiting from your Higher Self's wisdom for longer than you think.

CHAPTER

PUTTING IT ALL TOGETHER

Having begun all the exercises and the recommended mental processes, you are now ready to gather these experiences together and build a solid program for your new life direction. You may have noticed that I wrote "begun" the exercises. Most will bear repeating as they will continue to be helpful in your life. Building your program means pulling together all the information of the preceding chapters and creating an action plan for yourself. The plan must be specific as to times and days of the week for each activity and carried out with determination. Otherwise, when we are feeling low or tired, we have the tendency to put off activities for another day. This creates havoc with our program. A good idea is to write your daily plan and tape it next to your "refrigerator mantra" or perhaps take a page from your journal for it.

The only daily activity is twenty minutes to half an hour of meditation. If in the beginning you are having trouble meditating, use the time to sit quietly, as I suggested earlier. Probably at a later time you will find it easy to take the next little step toward regular meditation. Meditating in the morning is preferable as it will make your day more peaceful and will give you the energy to cope calmly and competently with the unexpected. In the evening you may be tired and stressed by the day's events and may fall asleep during your meditation. This is understandable but makes the meditation ineffective, especially if a Creative Visualization is part of your meditation.

At this point your capacity for self-discipline is really being challenged, as well as your personal commitment. Your Left Brain, (conscious) mind, is coming into play in creating a structured program with time and day specifications. As abiding by any structure is contrary to what the Right Brain (unconscious) would like to do, there will be resistance. This resistance may first show up during meditation when you find all sorts of busy thoughts passing through and distracting you from peaceful ones. The Right Brain would find it more fun letting things happen as they wish—"Let the chips fall where they may."

Trying to follow a process that demands more time and effort than you have to give will create stress, which will interfere with the positive effects of your program. Earlier in this book we talked about working within our limitations and adding a little extra task to put spice in our lives. In this case you don't need spice; you just need to feel capable and unthreatened. If it turns out that you do not look forward to your daily program and look for excuses to skip once in awhile, don't double up the following day because you feel guilty. In no way should you consider punishing yourself. The capacity to forgive oneself is a sign of progress in the process of liberation.

Take a look at your typical weekday and see if you can fit in your daily meditation. You may have to get up a half hour earlier, but the energizing effect of the meditation will easily make up for the "lost" half hour. If you can only meditate in the evening, you may have to go to bed half an hour later. In the evening, try meditating before dinner instead of just before going to bed. Meditating in the bedroom will make you sleepy, so sit in some other room. Without daily meditation, there is no point in trying to follow this program. Better to postpone the process until you are better able to devote the necessary time and energy.

Decide when you can make time to keep your journal up to date. You might also decide to contact your Higher Self on Sundays for suggestions. Prime your Probation Officer and make your first appointment. If friends are working with you, decide which exercises you can share and set the most convenient times.

What physical exercise do you need to do? Is there a gym nearby? Do you need a personal trainer? How many days can you go to the gym? If the often frantic atmosphere of the gym gets to you, you might rather exercise at home. Exercising at home is a real test of your self-discipline.

If you have been eating "take-out" fast food, you will now have to cook healthy meals at home. It may be that local health food stores are offering cooking classes. Join them, and if you have a live-in partner, have your partner join you in the classes. Cooking dinner together can be a fun time, particularly if you both work. Some health food stores have take-out dinners and will certainly have cookbooks for sale to help you. It may be that your health food store can recommend a nutritionist to design a healthy diet. If there is no one available locally, read up on nutritional foods and check the Internet. A nutritious diet is absolutely essential to maintaining a strong mind/body connection which can support your positive life changes. As I write this, there appeared in a health magazine a natural food service that prepares and delivers healthy meals to your home on a weekly basis. They apparently can ship meals to you regularly. There may be such a service in your area.

Elaine, a recently retired buyer for an Illinois department store chain, lived in Cleveland with her retired sister. Even though they had little in common and had had little contact over the years, living together made good sense. Combining their retirement incomes made it possible for them to live comfortably and travel once a year. Elaine's sister noticed in recent months a change in Elaine's voice and convinced her to seek medical advice. After a CAT scan and a biopsy, she was told that she had throat cancer. She had been a chain smoker since her teen years and an alcoholic most of her adult life. She was the kind of alcoholic that went on a binge once or twice a month and remained in control of her drinking the rest of the time.

Another reason for moving to Cleveland was because her daughter and three grandchildren lived nearby. She adored her three grandchildren and often gratefully accepted her daughter's invitation to baby sit. The oncologist whom she consulted invited Elaine into her office to let her try out an electric vibrator that when pressed against her throat allowed her to shape words with her lips and thus communicate. The operation would involve losing her voice. Her doctor told her that she ought to agree to have the operation as soon as possible as the cancer could be spreading. Elaine was horrified by the buzzing sound the vibrator made and was sure that it would terrify the youngest grandchild. The more she thought, the more she decided to find an alternative treatment.

One evening at dinner at a friend's house, she found herself sitting next to a soft-spoken Indian from Detroit, Michigan. He turned out to be a holistic practitioner with a clinic there. He spoke of his years of work with a variety of clients suffering from all sorts of illnesses, including AIDS, cancer, lupus and multiple sclerosis. Even after so many years of work, he said that he was still awed at the power of the mind over the body in the process of self-healing. Elaine became very excited and encouraged him to continue. She wondered if it was only a coincidence that they should find each other sitting side by side, particularly since she hadn't told her friend about her diagnosis. It appeared that some silent power in the universe had made it possible for them to meet.

The next week she phoned Dr. Patel and made an appointment for the following Thursday. He told her that she would have to be at his clinic by eight thirty in the morning as she would be going through several tests and interviews with different members of his staff. He told her quite honestly that her lifestyle, which included addiction to cigarettes and alcohol, might make it impossible to create a healthy internal environment for self-healing. If she was ready to go ahead with a program, she would have to make some immediate and drastic changes. Before any self-healing could take place, she would have to go through a detoxification program. She made the commitment to herself to do whatever was necessary. That evening she threw her cigarettes and lighter into the garbage and poured her bottle of whisky down the toilet. The following Thursday morning at six she was on the road.

Her first appointment was with a counselor who spent an hour explaining the principles of holistic philosophy and the commitments required. (Many of the steps she agreed to make were the same as listed in this book.) Her next appointment was with a specialist in relaxation, stress management and meditation. Together they practiced breathing from the diaphragm using yogic breathing techniques. She would have to remain conscious of her breathing and make sure that her intakes would begin by pushing her stomach forward before inflating her lungs. It would take a couple of months for her to breathe this way naturally without listening. An appointment was scheduled with a nutritionist who gave her the basic outline for a Macrobiotic Diet which she must strictly adhere to. This was part of the detoxification process. She was also given an herbal chelation regime to follow on a daily basis. In the late afternoon she met with Dr. Patel who had a computer printout of reports from the various meetings she had had during the day. She admitted to him that she felt exhausted but excited at the same time. Dr. Patel said he was encouraged by her demonstration of commitment and remained more optimistic than before.

To make a long story short, nine months later doctors could not find a trace of her cancer.

They sent her to the Mayo Clinic, which agreed that there was no evidence of active cancer in her throat. Her doctors, in an effort to explain their error in recommending standard protocol, called her recovery "an act of God."

Elaine demonstrated a great deal of courage in saying no to medical practitioners who created a sense of urgency and ensuing problems if she did not agree immediately to surgery. Today things are different as most doctors welcome a second opinion and are even willing to accept the benefits of some of the holistic treatments available.

Elaine was not prepared in advance for her meeting with the nutritionist. Try to make your appointment with a nutritionist a week in advance, thus giving you time to do your homework. Begin by keeping a log of all your meals for a week, including in-between meal snacks. Make a list of the foods you crave, that do not agree with you, and the foods that you cannot stand. List your allergies if you have any. Also think back and remember any chronic diseases which are common to your parents, such as diabetes and arthritis. Is obesity a family problem? All this information will help in creating your profile and dictate a diet and natural supplements for you, which will help you to achieve a high level of wellness.

EXERCISE

Now that we are moving forward, just by following the recommendations of this chapter is exercise enough.

CHAPTER 9

HAVE FUN!

During this process we tend to take ourselves too seriously; we then bore ourselves as well as our friends. This is quite natural as any project that requires much introspection and concentration does create a certain amount of personal tension. We can laugh at ourselves without being negative or threatening the process. We can laugh with others about our silly habits, idiosyncrasies and perceptions on life around us. The laughter should be spontaneous, not contrived. The laughing doesn't mean that we are going to give them up, instead we just accept them. Who's perfect?

Then there are those wonderful moments when a group gets together and begins to laugh to the point of weeping at anything. No matter what is said, it generates gales of laughter. This kind of near hysteria is good for us. The endorphins flow and we always feel better afterwards. "Have a good laugh or cry and you will feel better"—in both cases the endorphins flow and we will feel better for a while.

We want to steer clear of those "laugh therapists" who charge an entrance fee to participate in a laugh therapy hour, where everyone begins to force laughter which builds to such a pitch that it approaches group hysteria. It can be embarrassing to witness one hundred people screaming with forced laughter and watch the sadness and expressions of anxiety on their faces. They are anxious because they worry whether they are normal as they are not laughing on the inside. They do not want to disappoint the "laughter therapist" who seems like such a nice person. Laughter needs to be a spontaneous response to a funny happening.

Joseph Campbell's expression, "Follow your bliss," says it perfectly. What are we passionate about? Or in the vernacular, "What turns us on?" There must be a connection between our life purpose and our passion. Pursuing that passion creates a force that moves us forward in life with enthusiasm and excitement.

Honor your passion and integrate it into your new life. Find some way to experience it for at least part of your day. If you are interested in archeology, there are digs going on that you can participate in for your two-week vacation. If beekeeping is your passion, study all you can about bees. Find the nearest beekeeper and volunteer your help as beekeepers can always use another hand. If painting pictures is your passion, take lessons and join a local art society. What Campbell meant by "Follow your bliss" called for active participation, not just passive observation. If theatre is your passion, join a local amateur theatre group. If you are interested in collecting minerals and semi-precious gems, join a rock hound group and go on weekend trips.

If you like to make things with your hands and believe that they are marketable, make up a batch and take a booth at a crafts fair. This is a great spot to make friends.

I discussed earlier in this book the benefits of doing some volunteer work. Try to find volunteer opportunities in some way connected to your passion. Museums and art shows are always looking for guides to lead visitors around. Theatres need ushers and ticket sellers. Libraries need book sorters and storytellers for the "children's hour." If you like books, as someone in my community did, place an ad in the local classifieds announcing the beginning of a book club. Soccer and Little League teams are looking for coaches and Boy Scouts need adult counselors. Nonprofit community organizations need board members and fund raisers. This list is just to encourage you to do some creative thinking. Some newspapers run weekly notices of volunteer needs.

Finally, the greatest volunteer experience you can ever have is to give two years to volunteer work overseas. It will change your life forever and give you a new perspective on the world community and how you now connect with it. American Friends Service Committee, Mennonite Central Committee, Care Medico and International Rescue Committee are just a few opportunities. I don't recommend the U.S Peace Corps unless you are very supportive of our administration and its foreign policy. There is an Association of Voluntary Agencies, based in New York City, which is a good resource.

Create a group of new friends from your participation in community activities. Entertain these new friends in your home. If you are not sure you are up to cooking a whole meal, invite them for tea, drinks or dessert and coffee. Of course, they will wish to reciprocate and so begins a new social life with people with whom you share interests and passions.

Travel can also be fun, especially in countries whose cultures you are not familiar with. Study up on a country, learn a few useful words of the local language and try them out. The effort you make will be so appreciated whether you make mistakes or not.

I have traveled with friends and I have traveled alone. If you wish to immerse yourself in the local culture and meet local people, travel alone. People are much more likely to make contact if you are alone and may even invite you to their homes. Travel holding a dictionary and ask for the meaning of words in the local language. Showing a sincere interest in the local culture and spoken language will be very much appreciated. Warning! Don't fall into the trap of making comparisons between the local way and the American way. If you are asked, be vague in your response.

Romance can also be fun during this change process. Getting into long-term relationships is a mistake, but this does not mean you need to be celibate. The mistake can be that as you are going through this dynamic process your needs are changing. If a newfound partner seems to meet your present needs, a month later your needs may have changed and you regret having made a long-term commitment. Don't place expectations on your partner—just enjoy the moment.

EXERCISE

Actually the whole chapter is an exercise.

CHAPTER

10

A REVIEW

How can this chapter be most helpful to you? Are you feeling confused? Don't dump on yourself as we have covered a great deal of material so far. It seems to me that a brief summary of each chapter will help you remember some and to know which ones you need to look at again. The brief descriptions will save you from having to read the whole book over again. You need, however, to keep the book for some later rereading or for sharing with friends. Once they see your positive life changes, they will want to free themselves as well.

CHAPTER ONE, entitled "How Did I Get Here?" listed the different "bars" to your cell. Emphasis was on your values and perceptions. We talked about the need to take risks with confidence, to make a "leap of faith" and to accept responsibility for where you are and what you are doing. Begin to be comfortable with being your first priority. This is a prerequisite for liberation.

Here we also discuss the role of emotions and negative feelings which are keeping us in jail. When we are free of jail, we will know true happiness and won't delude ourselves, as many people do today, that money and spending will bring happiness. Happiness is not for sale.

We describe how negative feelings and emotions live in the Right Brain (unconscious) Long-Term Memory Bank. Here, there is a description of the exercise for clearing these negatives from the Memory Bank using Creative Visualization techniques.

Another "bar" is caused by negative friends and relationships. Is your cellmate holding you back? Suggestions for letting this person go are included.

CHAPTER TWO, entitled "Letting Go," teaches us how to let go and what that means. It shows us how our values can hold us back. We let go of the need to control others and events over which we have no control. We need to avoid creating unreasonable expectations of ourselves. We acknowledge our limitations, but set goals which demand just a bit more, thus adding some spice to our lives. Always succeeding in our goals leads us to complacency. Another letting-go step is to forgive others and let resentments go.

After reviewing your list of values, decide which are relevant to your new life and which are no longer appropriate. Let these go also. Remind yourself that you are now your own first priority. Discover and allow the person who you really are to appear. Never mind trying to meet others' expectations of you.

A series of physical changes follow, like buying a new car, finding a new job and changing your home. Then there is the commitment to spiritual growth which involves meditation, exercises found in this book, and possibly learning yoga exercises.

CHAPTER THREE is entitled "Moving On" and continues discussing some obstacles to doing just that. Impatience hampers the natural process of change. Take your time but still take risks. Another obstacle is a need to get even. Are we on this earth to punish those who have hurt us?

One of the most difficult obstacles is dealing with substance abuse. If this is a problem for us, we must address this problem head on. If we do not, then following the process of liberation becomes illusionary. In other words, we are playing mind games.

Fear of failure can be another block. When we acknowledge that we learn much more from our failures than successes, then we are moving forward in our search for wisdom. Willing to be vulnerable also offers us learning opportunities.

The final part asks that you begin writing your plan in your journal. Begin with the easier tasks.

CHAPTER FOUR is entitled "The Probation Officer." The first suggestion is to recruit a partner or two while you follow this plan. Often we can feel lonely and isolated as we move on. Next, choose a person who already appears liberated and ask them to become your Probation Officer to whom you will report once a month. This will be an opportunity to discuss the progress you are making and possible holdups you are facing.

In this chapter we strongly recommend that you let go of all negative friends. Some examples are listed, along with suggestions of the method for dumping them. Of course you guard and nurture your positive friends and associates.

Here you trust your "gut" feelings and avoid negative experiences and locations. We also urge that you avoid watching violent and negative movies and TV programs. We even suggest not watching television for a whole weekend.

The exercise at the end of the chapter was to list your negative qualities on one page and your positive ones on the facing page.

CHAPTER FIVE is entitled "Love Thyself"—how to build your self-esteem. Begin by taking time to acknowledge small accomplishments and victories. Here we suggest that you listen to the negative words you typically use, words that give you an "out" from moving on. Here are just some examples: "maybe I can," "perhaps," "I'll try," "fat chance" and "forget it." When you break something or make a mistake, don't you call yourself a "clumsy jerk" or "stupid ———"?

We discuss the fear of success problem which is often what challenges our self-esteem. This fear often begins during childhood. Now is the time to look at it and let it go. We are entitled to be successful.

Another destructive habit is what I call "rehearsing." We can spend hours, especially at night, reliving a past stressful situation or more often anticipating a difficult confrontation in the near future. It's almost as if we are on a fast merry-go-round and cannot get off. Rationalizing that we need our sleep more sometimes works. Think silently, STOP REHEARSING, and then roll over on your other side. If you sleep alone, say it out loud.

In this chapter we also explain in greater detail than before, the special meditation/visualization exercise for releasing chronic negative feelings which are spilling out from the Long-Term Memory in the Right Brain or unconscious.

At the end of this chapter there is an exercise. In your journal, list your negative perceptions of events that you have experienced in the past; now flip the coin and list what could have been positive lessons learned from these experiences. Once you have acknowledged these benefits, you will probably not have to face them again; and if you do, this time you will welcome them.

CHAPTER SIX is entitled "Who Needs Expectations?" We need to create expectations for ourselves—goals if you prefer. We do not invest any energy in fulfilling others' expectations of us, unless we do so voluntarily. An example might be to agree not to lick our knives at the dinner table, which we always did before we were married. The danger of expending all our energy meeting the expectations of others is that we no longer know who we really are. A good slogan is, "What you sees is what you gets!"

In a long-term relationship which has been maintained by each partner meeting the emotional needs of the other, the struggle for independence and self-realization is tough. This can be particularly painful if one partner is choosing to remain in jail. The partner remaining becomes very anxious as he or she faces having to take full responsibility for their life.

Creative Visualization can be used for achieving many goals, including fulfilling a vision of a wonderful life.

CHAPTER SEVEN is entitled "Meet Your Higher Self." In our process toward liberation and self-actualization, we need the support and guidance of our Higher Self or, if you will, inner voice or soul self. Whatever name we give it, it is the most powerful part of us. It is our source of wisdom and offers the best guidance in making important life decisions. The hunch or "ahaaas" most often come from our

Higher Self, which is why we must learn to trust our hunches and inspirations and not try to make them fit into a Left Brain or conscious logical or sensible frame. Children, who seem to be much more open to the Higher Self, often discuss them and wish to follow their recommendations. An adult usually interjects saying that they must learn not to trust them as they don't make any sense.

Another important role for the Higher Self is in its involvement in the healing process, particularly when we are faced with a serious illness. In this case it acts as a partner, advising on the necessary steps for spiritual healing, without which we can never be truly healed.

As the Higher Self depends upon the nonverbal Right Brain for communication, it has great difficulty using words. For this reason, using the *I-Ching*, an ancient Chinese oracle, as a means of communicating with the Higher Self has become most reliable. Carl Jung, the famous psychiatrist, used the *I-Ching* with his patients. Consulting it with a degree of reverence avoids frivolous and sometimes misleading responses. These come when we expect it to tell us what to do and ask it questions that expect a yes or no answer. Since this oracle is a source of wisdom, it does not belong on a coffee table nor is it to be consulted frequently. The ideal question might be to ask for a new perspective on a problem and even advice on the sequence of steps to be taken. What continues to mind-boggle its users is that the answers always seem so very appropriate to the situation at hand.

Daily meditation or silence offers us an opportunity to ask advice from our Higher Self. The answer will often come in image form. Its interpretation will be like interpreting dreams and will require some reflection.

Finally, the Higher Self becomes the channel for

launching out requests to the universe for the fulfillment of specific goals. The exercise at the end of this chapter is to reflect on the important life decisions you have made in the past and how you came to make them. Was it by "gut feeling"? (Does our Higher Self live in our gut?)

CHAPTER EIGHT is entitled "Putting It All Together." It is time to create your program. The only firm daily commitment is to meditate or sit still each day. Other exercises and experiments may be scattered throughout the week at convenient times.

Here you don't set goals that you cannot possibly achieve. (Not too much spice this time.) Acknowledge your time and energy limitations. A good test for your program is that if you do not look forward to working your program, then you have set too much on your platter.

Set up a weekly exercise program. Consult a trainer if you need to. Follow up with an appointment with a nutritionist and cook tasty meals that are good for you. Contrary to common opinion, healthy food can be delicious. Before this consultation, keep a record of all you have eaten for a week and also make a list of foods you crave and that you believe you are allergic to.

CHAPTER NINE is entitled "Have Fun!" We tend to take ourselves too seriously during such a program. We need to learn to laugh at our silly habits and idiosyncrasies. Who's perfect, after all? Always let the laughter be spontaneous and not forced. Stay away from workshops offered by "laughter therapists" who charge admission for paying participants to sit around and laugh hysterically together. Watching these workshops on television is depressing as the expression on the faces of many of the participants shows more sadness and anxiety than natural joy.

Joseph Campbell's recommendation to "Follow your bliss" is the best way to say "experience your passion." Try to find some time in your day or at least in your week to do something that turns you on. Honor your passion. I believe it is in some way connected to our life purpose. Another joy comes from being needed. Volunteer work fulfills that need.

Other fun things to do might include entertaining new friends, learning to cook, travel and taking courses. Above all, don't give up romance; just be wise in how you handle it. Until you actually feel self-actualized, avoid long-term commitments.

I hope that these summaries will help you to move on. You need to realize that the process does not stop on a certain day, but becomes an integral part of an exciting lifetime experience.

CREATIVE VISUALIZATION

Creative Visualization is not a new New Age technique. It's been used for thousands of years and is used naturally by children today. Actually it was invented by Neanderthal man to help him become a greater hunter. My wife and I discovered this when we visited the Lascaux Caves in central France. He selected the innermost cave of a series to house his family. There the natural ground heat, combined with the heat from torches and the barbecue, made it possible for his family members to shed their furs and lay about naked. This was all the incentive he needed to invent "Febreze." In preparing to go out on the hunt, he would grab a bunch of spears. He needed the spares because sometimes a spear would become embedded in the rear end of a fleeing Mastodon. Okay, let's get serious. As he walked through the caves, carrying his spears to the first cave, he would pause before each wall painting where he had depicted himself in stick-figure form spearing an animal at least fifty times bigger than himself. The flickering flame of the torch made the scene even more real. By the time he had reached the entrance cave, he would be so fired up that he knew he was invincible and that his lazy family would eat again soon.

Children use the technique naturally in dealing with their daily problems. Adults call it fantasizing and look down on it as if it were some manifestation of a mental deficiency.

We have since discovered that doing it naturally can have some healing benefits. And we do have the expression, "Dreams become reality," which we use without apology.

Taking the fantasy one step forward using specific techniques, we can now use it with confidence to achieve goals. The fantasy does not produce results if it lacks persistence and frequency. If we have not taken the time to learn the steps to the creation of the visualization or vision and how to present it to the Right Brain, we will become discouraged and say, "Creative Visualization will never work for me!"

I have been using Creative Visualization with individuals and groups for more than thirty years with success. I am pleased to read in the press today that its effectiveness has been given some legitimacy. Last August an essay written by Barbara Ehrenreich appeared in *The New York Times Book Review* entitled "Who Moved My Ability to Reason?" In it she emphasizes the importance of maintaining a positive attitude and how negative attitudes "can be harmful to your health and might even shorten your lifespan." She refers to the book, *Secrets of the Millionaire Mind*, which cites that your thoughts can alter the physical universe and that there "is akin to a big mail-order department" in which you "order" what you want. She quotes a 2001 book, *The Ultimate Secret to Getting Absolutely Everything You Want*, which states that thoughts exert a gravitational-type force on the world so that "whenever you think something, the thought immediately attracts its physical equivalent." Author Ehrenreich also discusses thinking and using victim words.

Some of the uses of Creative Visualization include:

healing the body and mind, stress management, cleansing accumulated negative energies from the Long-Term Memory Bank (exercise described in chapters one and three), achieving life goals, fulfilling one's passion, healing pain and sadness, and finding the ideal job and place to live.

In the area of body/mind/spirit healing, I am reminded of a professor in the Midwest who needed a liver transplant. He had been on a waiting list for several months for a donated liver and his condition was critical. When a liver was finally matched and the operation took place, his family was relieved, particularly his three young children who had been carefully prepared for his passing. When he came home, there was a family celebration. He was told that he would need to take anti-rejection drugs for the rest of his life. A week later he began behaving strangely, especially at night while lying in bed. He would have outbursts of sobbing without any logical reason. The frequency of his crying increased until, at the suggestion of his brother, he agreed to make an appointment with me. After a couple of hours together, we discovered that the crying was caused by his mourning the loss of his old liver. Here we have to recognize that experiencing any kind of organ transplant generates many uncommon responses and emotional reactions. It became clear to me that this situation could be treated by creating a visualization to be used in combination with a program of daily meditation.

After twenty minutes of meditation, he imagined the following scenes. The first scene takes place at the cemetery where the old liver is lowered into the ground with accompanying prayers by the local pastor. As the hired limousine turns down the professor's street, he is amazed to see numbers of cars in front of his house. When he steps out of the limousine, he hears dance music coming from the back terrace. His wife rushes out to greet him and explains that they are having a welcoming party for his new liver. The professor lived for more years than is typical of liver transplant recipients. After receiving Christmas cards from him for three years, I lost touch. If he has died, I know that his children loved each year he remained with them.

Another example of visualization is a CD that I designed to reduce, and in some cases completely eliminate the negative side effects of chemotherapy. The results have been amazing.

Using Creative Visualization in stress management will be described in that section.

Now you may be getting impatient with me because I still haven't told you how to do it. It is important to know how we believe the process works. If we have written a letter to Santa Claus, there is a slim chance of receiving our request. If, however, we send out a thought form through our Higher Self, the chances are much better. Specifically, when we create a vision or image of what we desire with our conscious mind which is verbal and transfer it to our unconscious or Right Brain which is nonverbal—when it is most receptive (during meditation)—it translates the image into a nonverbal vision which may then be launched into the universe by the Higher Self. This transfer is carried on one of the many channels of communication that we are not consciously aware of. We wonder why repeating the same words, over and over again, does not work as efficiently. The answer is that the Right Brain or unconscious is nonverbal and prefers images. We have read in the past of teachers making a chronically late student write on the blackboard, "I will not be late for school" three hundred times. By creating an image of the child running through the entrance of the school, looking up at the clock over the door which reads five to nine, and asking the child to spend five minutes of classroom time in the morning imaging the scene will do just as well.

Let's begin our visualization. Here are some "dos and don'ts" to commit to before beginning.

1. Have complete faith in the system. Any doubt will interfere with the necessary communication.

2. Set no time limits or times for the fulfillment of the goals. (They will arrive when you are ready, not before.)

3. Use as many descriptions of sensory impressions as possible (smell, sound, texture, temperature and taste).

4. If you change your mind or goal, be sure to send out a cancellation; otherwise you will receive what you no longer wish for.

5. Keep the image foremost in your mind. During the day when you are doing a task that doesn't require much attention, like vacuuming or mowing the lawn, bring forth the image. The more you do, the stronger the message going out in the universe.

6. Always focus on the goal as having been accomplished, not the process. The process for achieving the goal will take care of itself.

7. Don't judge the visualization as being crazy or too way out, just keep on working.

Write your visualization keeping in mind number three above. Do not be too detailed.

You are not writing a short story. Make it simple enough so that it will be easy to imagine with your eyes closed during your meditation or with your eyes open while you are cutting grass or washing dishes.

You may have to try a few times for the system to work. Begin by setting simple goals that have a good chance of achievement. Then move up to the more complicated.

I repeat that the most efficient way to get into your Right Brain is during meditation.

THE GOOD AND BAD STRESS

We often think of the word "stress" as a negative. What makes it good or bad is the degree of it that we are coping with. Good stress is very supportive of our basic instinct for survival. Without it we might not look both ways before crossing the street. We might not react with sufficient adrenalin to run away from an angry hive of African killer bees. Stress becomes destructive when we are sitting anxiously in our living room imagining that when we later go to the garden we might be attacked by a swarm of angry bees. Fear plays a big role in destructive stress.

Destructive stress is the theme of this section. How to recognize it and what are its symptoms? This section is not designed to treat your stress, as that would take much more space than we have here. We will, however, discuss some steps you might wish to take to reduce it.

It appears that there are two kinds of stress: environmental and internal. In most cases we cannot remove or change environmental stress factors as they are beyond our control. What we can do is to change our perception of the cause or through rationalization agree that they will continue to exist in spite of us. The finest example of this is the weather. Here the media weather persons seem to take some sadistic pleasure in making normal weather into disaster predictions and elevating our stress levels. I believe the plan here is to take some viewers away from the competition. If we have to drive to work after a "disastrous" snowstorm, we become so stressed that our driving and limited reflexes make us a threat to all the other drivers going to work. In fact, some accidents can be attributed to these media sadists. Other environmental stressors may include noisy neighbors; if talking to them doesn't work, then a move may be in order. Under no circumstances should you hire a witch to put a curse on them as curses can backfire.

Another stress which has gripped a majority of citizens of our country is the threat of terrorist acts. What makes it so stressful is that its occurrence, type, location and time are unpredictable. Feeling powerless to deal with a disaster, and in some cases protect our families, raises and maintains a constant high level of stress. Besides the obvious things we can do, such as providing our children with cell phones and asking them to check in regularly, we can bring the family spiritually closer together, do more activities together and eat together more often. In other words, the family becomes a spiritual support system which helps members to detach from the outside and creates a greater sense of inner security.

Next to terrorism, the increasing local crime rate appears almost manageable. House and car alarms, neighborhood watches and avoidance of dangerous areas all give us confidence.

The work place offers some choice stressors. We will not take the space here to list many of them, but one of the most common is "the Boss." We have had some success in the past helping clients deal with this stress, using Creative Visualization to help them change their negative perceptions and look at that person from a different angle.

Managing and reducing internal stress is easier. Here, the individual has control, providing he or she has made the commitment to deal with it. The source of most of the internal stress issues rise up from the Long-Term Memory Bank which sits in the Right Brain. These include chronic negative feelings which are so intense that they appear to intrude in our life situations whether they are appropriate or not. Some examples might include chronic feelings of guilt which drive us to satisfy others' needs before dealing with our own. A chronic feeling of anger gives us the sensation that we have an angry bear looking over our shoulder. Again, experiencing a positive event can still bring up the urge of anger, even though there is no way to justify its emergence. Other chronic feelings might include fear and emotional pain. Recalling past traumatic and painful experiences, such as abuse, betrayal, loss, abandonment and loss of face, can add to the stress burden.

What are some of the symptoms of an overload of stress of both kinds, such as feeling trapped, abused, taken for granted, exploited or out of control? Inability to maintain a healthy relationship without dependencies, low self-esteem, squabbling with close family members, living day by day without planning for the future, forgetful (where did I put my car keys?) and a whole litany of physical illnesses, the majority being autoimmune diseases such as arthritis, lupus, migraine-like headaches, bad backs, frequent colds and sinus infections. When the immune system's energy is distracted from its normal function of maintaining our wellness in order to deal with the surges of adrenalin in our body, something has to give. A stress response of extra doses of adrenalin, accompanied by our own produced corticol, is manifested to give us more hormonal energy to deal with the perceived crisis. The corticol (our own manufactured cortisone) kills millions of antibodies as it flows through our body, making us much more vulnerable to illness.

Most of us who don't know how to deal with an overload of stress have found patterns of behavior that only give temporary relief. These include overuse of prescription drugs, chain smoking, alcohol and illegal drug abuse, risk taking, fast driving, excessive sleeping, depression, gambling, "workaholism" and overeating.

Some of the positive things we can do to deal with an overload of stress are exercise, including walking and yoga, meditation combined with Creative Visualization, and a healthy diet which avoids greasy foods and many sweets.

Working with a specialized therapist can be very helpful. Attending a stress management meeting with a large group of participants will only teach you how to relax. Managing your stress can only be dealt with on a one-on-one basis. Each of us has our special set of stress factors.

ACKNOWLEDGMENTS

To Carlo Clavi, Maggie Nolan, Kit Johnston, Oscar Torres, Betty Dew and John Saccu who took the time to read and comment on the first draft. Special thanks to Joan Johnson for volunteering to edit the manuscript and to Emly McDiarmid who made many very helpful suggestions for improving the manuscript. To Maria Rodriguez and Carmen Lydia Rodriguez for making available an apartment on the Caribbean shore in Puerto Rico where the first draft was written. Finally, to friends and clients who encouraged me to write this book.

Printed in the United States
145688LV00001B/60/A